You Make The Difference

In Helping Your Child Learn

by Ayala Manolson M.Sc Speech Language Pathologist
with Barb Ward M.Ed Special Educator
and Nancy Dodington BA. Family Support Worker

Illustrations by Robin Baird Lewis
Cartoons by Lee Rapp
Cover & Title Pages by Ilana Manolson

You Make the Difference® in Helping Your Child Learn
By Ayala Manolson, Barbara Ward and Nancy Dodington

 The
Hanen
Centre®

A Hanen Centre Publication

The Hanen Centre, The Parent-Child Logo and You Make the Difference® are trademarks owned by Hanen Early Language Program

© Hanen Early Language Program, 2007
First Edition

Library and Archives Canada Cataloging in Publication

ISBN 978-0-921145-06-6

Copies of this book may be ordered from the publisher:

The Hanen Centre
1075 Bay Street, Suite 515
Toronto, ON
Canada M5S 2B1

Telephone: (416) 921-1073
Fax: (416) 921-1225
Email: info@hanen.org
Web: www.hanen.org

Parts of this book were adapted from It Takes Two To Talk™ — A Parent's Guide to Helping Children Communicate, a Hanen Centre publication. Copyright 1983 by Hanen Early Language Program. Revised 1984, 1985, 1992, 2004.

Illustrations: Robin Baird Lewis & Lee Rapp
Cover & Title pages: Illana Manolson

Printed in Canada by Thistle Printing

I believe the children are our future.
Teach them well, and let them lead the way,
Show them all the beauty they possess inside,
Give them a sense of pride to make it easier,
Let the children's laughter remind us of how we used to be.

Linda Creed

Thanks to the many people who have influenced and encouraged the writing of this book.

- Derek Nelson, past president of the Hanen Centre, for believing in our dream to provide community based prevention programs and for creatively finding the funds to support it.

- The parents, children and staff who participated in our pilot projects in the housing developments at Tobermory, Falstaff and Jessie's Centre for Teenagers. They taught us to talk straight and encouraged us to tell other parents what they should know about helping children learn.

- William Manolson for his constant caring and his wise advice.

- Dr. Marc Lewis for sharing his knowledge of mother-child interactions. His sensitive and insightful directions were invaluable in the creation of Chapter 10.

- Helen Buck, dear friend, for her insistence on clarity and for her gift with words and rhyme.

- Andy Hurlbut for his care and ability in the graphic design of this book. Only his gentle patience could have seen us through the many many revisions of this book.

- To our colleagues who so generously gave of their time and expertise to review the final draft of this book. Elaine Weitzman, Claire Watson, Jerry Newton, Dr. Monte Bail, Frith Manolson, Harold Hanen, Dr. Maria Erickson, Joanne Grey, Cindy Earle, Dr. Louis Rossetti, Dr. Gail Donahue, Dr. Alice Kahn, Michelle Craig, Judy Ball, Kerry Proctor-Williams, Rhona Wolpert, Mary Manning, Lamont Johson, Jane Bisantz, Carol Jenkins, Diane Eynon, Paula Moss, Leslie Suite, Patricia Chambers and Karen Ward. Their comments and support have really made a difference.

- Jessie's Centre for Teenagers for allowing Nancy Dodington to devote time to this project.

— for financial assistance:

- The men and women who work in Toronto's Bay Street financial community who contributed to the Bay Street Invitational Golf Tournament. Their generous funding supported the development and implementation of the Caring Connections Project and this book.

- Ilana Manolson who supported this project by donating her artwork.

- Le Château Stores of Canada, who helped finance the cartoons in this book.

Table of Contents

You Make the Difference

in helping your child learn

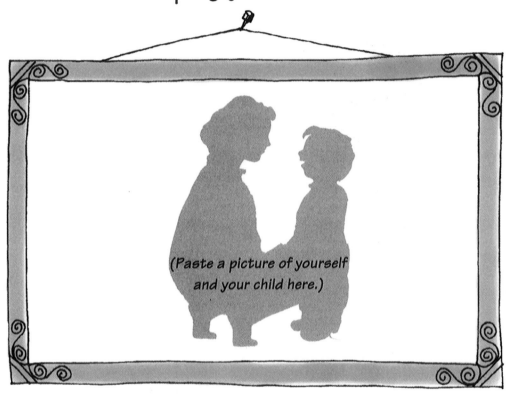

(Paste a picture of yourself
and your child here.)

You know your child best and care about him the most.
You want to help him grow up to be the best he can be.
It's important to remember that
HOW you connect with your young child affects:

- how he feels about himself
- his chances to learn.

How you connect with your child makes the difference

When you're THE HELPER

You want to make things easier and faster for your child.

But when you help too often, your child misses chances to learn.

When you're RUSHED

You are trying to get so much done.

But when you're in a hurry, you don't have time to talk to your child in ways that help her learn.

When you're THE TEACHER

You're the one doing most of the talking.

But your child learns best by doing, not only by being told what to do.

Now, you listen to me.

When you NEED A BREAK

You're tired or frustrated and want a break.

But if you take breaks too often when your child really wants to be with you, you'll miss some of the best times for sharing and learning.

How you connect with your child makes the difference

When you're THE TUNED-IN PARENT

You take the time to get to know your child and share his experiences. Your child feels recognized and special.

When you are tuned-in, your child feels good about himself and is open to learning.

The TUNED-IN PARENT goes through the day the 3a WAY!

The 3**a** WAY means

allow
your child to lead

adapt
to share the moment

add
new experiences and words

It's hard to be the TUNED-IN PARENT all the time.

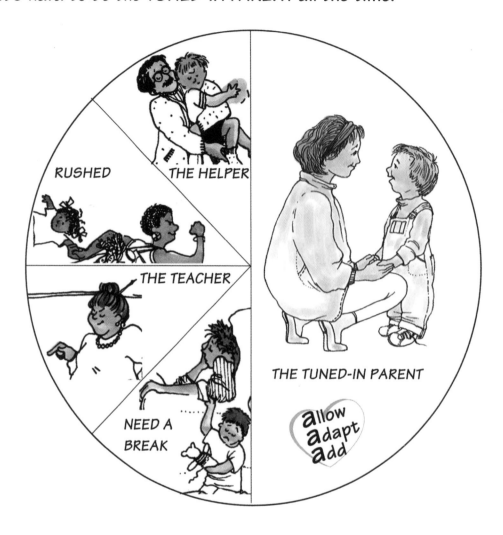

RUSHED

THE HELPER

THE TEACHER

NEED A BREAK

THE TUNED-IN PARENT

**allow
adapt
add**

But, the more time you can be the TUNED-IN PARENT, the happier your child will be and the more chances he will have to learn.

This book explains how the 3a WAY can help you tune-in to your child while you do all the things you usually do during the day.

allow Your Child to Lead

When you allow your child to lead:
- you give your child the chance to explore and learn
- you get to know your child better
- you help your child gain confidence

allowing your child to lead means taking a moment to . . .

allow
adapt
add

Observe . . . what your child is interested in and feeling

Wait . . . to see what your child will do

Listen . . . to your child and hear what he is trying to tell you

These three very important words — OBSERVE, WAIT and LISTEN — can be remembered by their first letters: OWL.

Taking the time to OWL is wise!

 **O**bserve

NOTICE what your
child is looking at . . .

WATCH the look on
your child's face . . .

LOOK AT your child's
body language

Sometimes it's hard to really know what is on your child's mind. But taking the time to OBSERVE will help you figure it out. Observing is the first and most important step in getting to know your child.

Wait

When you WAIT, you give your child the time
he needs to try things on his own.

WAITING is hard to do. Sometimes you have to count to ten — then
your child may say or do something that will surprise you.

O**W****L**isten

When you LISTEN, you will hear
what your child wants to tell you.

The only way to know what's on your child's mind is to LISTEN.
You can't listen if you're talking.

What to Observe, Wait and Listen for as your child develops

In the beginning,
you try to figure out what your child wants, needs or doesn't like when she:

- smiles, coos, cries in a special way
- looks uncomfortable or startled
- looks at something or turns away

Then,
when she's a little older, it's easier for you to follow her lead because she:

- begins to explore her world and shows you what she wants
- smiles when you copy her sounds and begins to copy yours
- understands a few words like "up", "daddy" and "bottle"

Later,

your child lets you know
what he wants when he:

- imitates your sounds
  and actions
- takes turns when you play
  simple games like peek-a-boo
- tugs at you, points, makes
  sounds, then looks back
  to see if you're watching
- makes sounds that you
  recognize as words

ba ba

Butterfly! Yes, Ashraf, that's a butterfly!

Boofly!

A butterfly, Katie. A pretty butterfly!

Still later,

it's a lot easier to know what she's
interested in because she:

- can use some words and short
  sentences (some words may be
  hard for you to understand)
- explores and tries new things
- may ask simple questions

**Finally, your child really begins to talk,
and then there's no stopping her!**

When you OBSERVE, WAIT and LISTEN, and then follow her lead,
she'll surprise and delight you with all she can do and say.

ALL IN A DAY!

Follow your child's lead in everyday life:

Instead of scowling . . .   *Try OWL-ing.*

Instead of butting in . . .   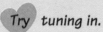 *Try tuning in.*

Instead of taking over . . .

Try tuning in.

Instead of thinking you know . . .

Try letting your child go.

I Took His Hand and Followed

My dishes went unwashed today
I didn't make my bed
I took his hand and followed
Where his eager footsteps led.

Oh yes, we went adventuring
My little child and I
Exploring all the great outdoors
Beneath the sun and sky.

We watched a robin feed her young
We climbed a sunlit hill
Saw cloud-sheep scamper through the sky
We plucked a daffodil.

That my house was so neglected
That I didn't brush the stairs
In twenty years no one on earth
Will know or even care.

But that I've helped my little child
To noble adulthood grow
In twenty years the whole wide world
May look and see and know.

Author unknown

CHAPTER THREE

adapt to Share the Moment

When you adapt to "Share the Moment":
- you let your child know that you're interested in him
- your child pays more attention to what you do or say
- you feel closer to your child and he feels closer to you
- you have more fun together

How to Share the Moment

You help your child "Share the Moment" when you . . .

Play face to face

Imitate

A hole.

Interpret

Wet.

Comment

KIDS WANT EQUAL TURNS

Take turns

What will Dolly wear?

Ask questions

Play Face to Face

Change your position so that your child
can look right into your eyes.

When you are face to face:
- you learn more about your child
- your child learns more from you
- you connect and share the moment

How to Share the Moment

Imitate – Copy your child's actions and sounds

Do what your child does.
Say what your child says.

When you imitate your child's sounds and actions:
- you connect with your child easily
- your child knows that you are interested in what he does and says
- your child may imitate you

Interpret – Say it as your child would if she could

Uh-oh!

Yeah, a HOLE! A big HOLE!

Put in a word that explains what is happening.

When you interpret:
- you let your child know you are trying to understand her
- you give your child words to help her learn to talk

How to Share the Moment

**Comment – talk about
what's happening**

A simple comment can work like magic
to start a conversation!

When you comment:
- you let your child know that you're interested
- you can tell your child new and interesting things
- you can start a conversation in an easy, gentle way

Ask questions – keep the conversation going

Ask a question that your child understands and wants to answer. Then wait for an answer.

When you ask questions that keep conversations going:
- you encourage your child to think
- your child knows you are interested

How to Share the Moment

Take Turns

A good conversation is like a good seesaw ride:
It happens only when each partner keeps taking a turn!

When you take turns with your child:
- she has a chance to express herself — even if it's just
  a smile, a giggle or a wiggle
- the more chances your child has to take a turn,
  the more chances she'll have to learn.

ALL IN A DAY!
Sharing the Moment in everyday life

Instead of talking to the wall . . . *Try giving your child a call.*

Instead of giving directions . . . *Try giving choices.*

ALL IN A DAY!

Instead of scaring . . .  Try sharing.

Instead of grilling . . . Be willing to wait for the answer.

add New Experiences
and Words

First comes experience, then understanding, and finally words.

When you add Experiences and Words:
- you help your child learn about his world
- you give your child the words he'll say when he is ready

How to **a**dd New Experiences and Words

allow
adapt
add

The world can be confusing.
You help your child learn when you . . .

Use actions

Give it a name

Imitate and add
a word or action

Make the important
words stand out

Repeat, repeat, repeat

Add a new idea

Use Actions

Try using your body to show your child
what your words are saying.

When you use actions and words at the same time:
- you make the message clearer
- you get your child's interest
- you give your child a way to tell you something,
  even when he doesn't have the words

How to **a**dd New Experiences and Words

Give Your Child a Word for It

Give names to things you do and see.

You help your child understand and learn when you give him a word for:
- what he's interested in
- what you are doing
- what just happened or will happen

Copy what your child does or says,
then add another word or action.

When you imitate and add a word or action:
- you build on what your child already knows
- you give your child new information she can understand
- you give your child another word to use when she is ready

How to **a**dd New Experiences and Words

Emphasize the important words.

When you highlight the words that matter:
- it's easier for your child to hear and remember them
- you make new words more interesting

Repeat, Repeat, Repeat

Find as many different ways as possible
to use the same actions or words

You may have to say it 10 times or 100 times.
But when you repeat:

- you help your child understand and remember new words
- your child will be able to use new words when she is ready

How to **a**dd New Experiences and Words

Add a New Idea

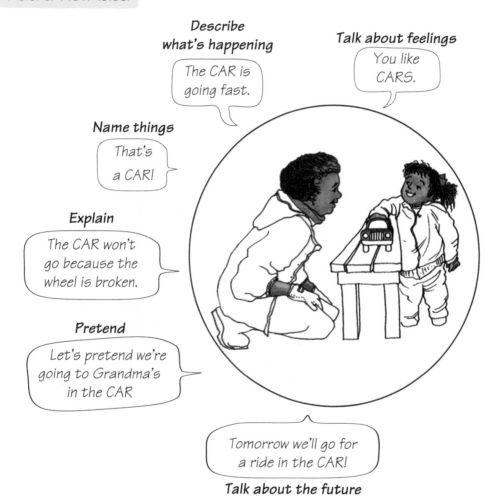

Describe what's happening

The CAR is going fast.

Talk about feelings

You like CARS.

Name things

That's a CAR!

Explain

The CAR won't go because the wheel is broken.

Pretend

Let's pretend we're going to Grandma's in the CAR

Tomorrow we'll go for a ride in the CAR!

Talk about the future

When you add a new idea you:
- build on the actions and words she already knows
- help your child understand the world
- give her a new way of thinking and talking

In the circle below draw a picture of something your child likes to do. Then write down what you could say to help your child learn more. (Keep in mind what your child is able to understand.)

Describe what's happening

_____

_____

Name things

_____

_____

Talk about feelings

_____

_____

Explain

_____

_____

Talk about the future

_____

_____

Pretend

_____

_____

Because your child is special in his very own way and so are you, it will take time to figure out ways that feel right for both of you. Don't simply read through this book. Keep trying out the ideas. Your child will let you know when you've got it right.

ALL IN A DAY!
adding experiences and words in everyday life

Instead of saying "that" or "this" . . . *Try giving a word that he can't miss.*

Instead of letting a chance go by . . . *Try giving info on the fly.*

Instead of testing, testing, testing . . . Try saying something interesting.

Instead of shaming . . . **Try** naming.

REMEMBER . . .
The Tuned-In Parent connects the 3**a** WAY

allow
adapt
add

allow Your Child to Lead

adapt to Share the Moment

add New Words and Experiences

The 3a WAY
to Play

When you're the tuned-in parent
You play the 3a WAY,
Your child will have the chance to learn
And . . . all the fun of play.

The way you play makes the difference!

... and then the King said ...

When you're THE ENTERTAINER

You put on a show and your child just watches you.

But if your child doesn't get a turn, he won't get a chance to learn.

That block, Julie! Put it on top! Now get a red one!

When you're THE DIRECTOR

You show and tell your child how to play and what to do.

But if you take over, your playmate might take off.

When you're THE REPORTER

You talk about what's happening instead of joining in the play.

But if all you do is talk,
your child may decide to walk.

You're crawling way under the table.

When you're THE WATCHER

You watch your child play but you don't get involved.

But if you are not really there it is impossible to share.

The way you play makes the difference!

When you're the TUNED-IN PARENT you play the 3a WAY . . .

You **a**dapt the play to share the fun.

You **a**dd new ways to play.

Your child learns more.

You **a**llow your child to choose what to play.

You get to know your child better.

Your child learns to take turns.

Your child feels important.

When you play the 3a WAY, you both have more fun.

allow
adapt
add

Your child can play with more than you'll find in a toy store . . .

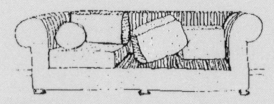

It's amazing how many things a sofa can be!

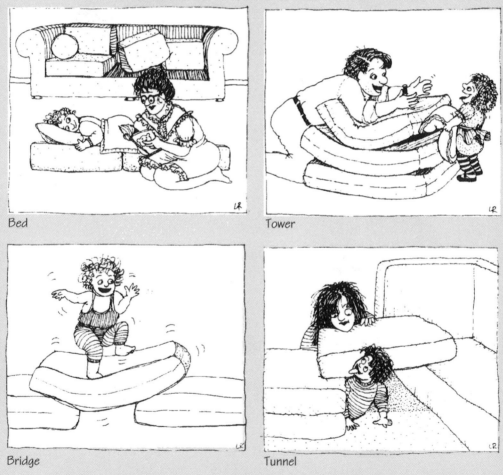

Bed

Tower

Bridge

Tunnel

When you tune-in the 3a WAY,
Life opens up to all kinds of play.

The next part of the book shows you how
to play the 3a WAY when you . . .

Go With Games

Make the Most
of Music

Get Hooked
on Books

Create, Create –
Don't Hesitate

Go with Games

When you play games the 3a WAY, you help your child:
- learn actions and sounds — even before she can talk
- get better at taking turns and taking chances
- discover the fun of pretending
- learn to get along with others

Playing Games the 3a WAY

allowing your child to lead in games means . . .
taking the time to OBSERVE, WAIT and LISTEN

Observing

your child lets you know if he's
interested or not.

If your child looks away, shakes
his head, or wanders off, try
something else.

Waiting

gives your child a chance to
join in . . . his way.

Listening

carefully to your
child makes him
feel special.

allowing your child to lead means thinking like a kid . . . YOUR kid!

YOU are the best toy in the house when you . . . **a**llow **a**dapt **a**dd

Playing Games the 3a WAY

adapting to Share the Moment in games means . . .

*Mommy's hand.
Baby's hand.*

Play face to face

Pat-a-cake

Imitate

Help your child
copy your actions

Interpret

Say what your child
would say if she
could talk, then . . .

Oooo

*Oooo! It's going
to fall!*

Wait

for her
to take
her turn

Recognize how your child takes a turn

In the beginning,
your child's turn is a giggle,
a wiggle, or just looking at you
in games like "gonna getcha"
and "peek-a-boo".

Later,
your child can clearly let you
know that she wants the game
to continue.

Still later,
after many, many repetitions,
your child will start the game
and want you to join in.

And finally,
your child will know how to play the whole game.

Playing Games the 3a WAY

adding new experiences and words in games means . . .

Use gestures
and make the
important words
stand out.

> Baby's
> SLEEPING.
> Ssshhh!

> Shhh!

Imitate and add
a word or action

> Yummy
> DONUT!

> Do-na!

Repeat, repeat, repeat

Build on what your child knows

Game Suggestions

Pots and Pans

Nursery Rhymes

Games with Balls

Games with Blocks

Card Games

Hide and Seek

Dress-up

Chapter Six

Make the Most of Music

Music has the power to comfort, relax and entertain.

Sharing music the 3a WAY helps your child:

- listen – the rhythm gets his attention
- learn new words and actions
- discover the fun of singing and dancing

Making the most of music the 3a WAY

allowing your child to lead in music means . . .
taking the time to OBSERVE, WAIT and LISTEN

At first,

your child may move to the beat of the music. When you stop singing and wait, he will let you know if he wants more by bouncing or swaying.

Then,

after you've sung a favorite song many times, your child may try to imitate your actions.

If you're happy and you know it . . .

Later,
when you pause during the song,
your child may try to fill in the
actions and words.

Finally,
your child will sing the
song all by himself.
Hooray!

Allow your child to sing the song in his own way.

Making the most of music the 3**a** WAY

adapting to share music means . . .

Sing face to face

Interpret

your child's sounds and
help her learn new songs

Pause

and let your
child take a turn

Slow down

so your child can really
hear the words

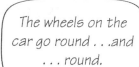

Making the most of music the 3a WAY

adding new experiences and words in music means . . .

Make the important words stand out

Repeat, repeat, repeat

Use actions and gestures

Make songs part
of your daily routine

Music Suggestions

CHAPTER SEVEN

Get Hooked on Books

Sharing books the 3a WAY helps your child:
- learn to pay attention
- find out about the world
- get ready for learning at school

The right book for the right time . . .

**Children will enjoy and learn from books
in different ways at different ages**

At first,

your baby believes books taste better
than they look.

Cloth and cardboard books are the safest.

Later,

your child will like books with
pictures he can "feel" and "smell"
or "do things with."

Then,
your child likes to
see and name things
she knows.

Duck . . .

Still later,
your child chooses her favorite
book from the shelf and brings
it to you.

Reading books the 3**a** WAY

allow your child to lead with books by taking the time to . . .

Observe

what your child does
with a book.

Wait

Your child may look at one
page for a long time.

When your child knows the
story, you can wait and let
him tell you part of it.

Listen

carefully to the
sounds or words
your child makes . . .

Ba-ba

. . . And then Follow his Lead!

It's OK just to talk about the pictures.

It's OK to change the words.

It's OK to put your child's name in the story.

It's even OK to read the last page first

— or any page that interests your child . . .

And of course it's OK to read a favorite book over and over again.

Remember to . . . *allow* *adapt* *add*

Reading books the 3a WAY

adapting to share with books means . . .

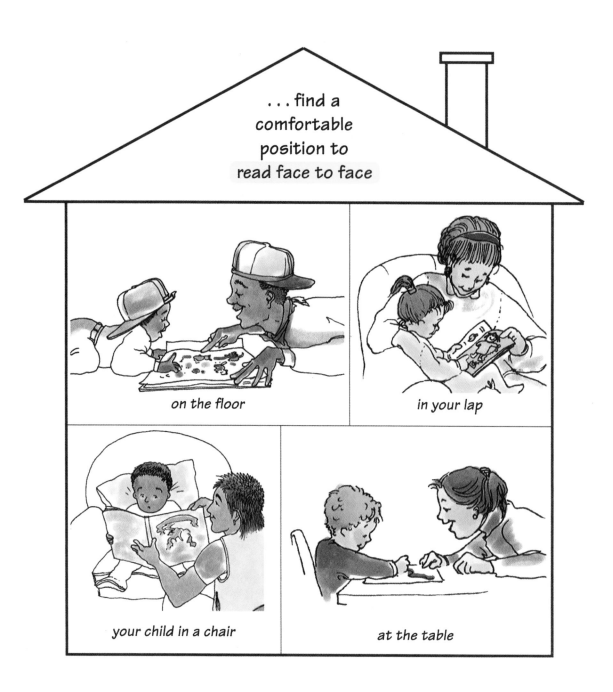

. . . find a
comfortable
position to
read face to face

on the floor

in your lap

your child in a chair

at the table

Take Turns

with your child.

Imitate and Interpret

your child's sounds
and actions.

Reading books the 3a WAY

adding new experiences and words
while sharing books means . . .

**Imitate and add
a word or action**

**Make the words
come to life**

Repeat, repeat, repeat

The PHONE. We talked to Gramma on the PHONE. It's fun to talk on the PHONE!

Add a new idea

Now, do you want to PHONE daddy?

Reading together gives you a quiet cozy time with something to look at and talk about.

Homemade books and made-up stories delight your child and help him learn

Make your own books . . .

A picture book
of things your child likes: firetrucks, faces or frogs!

It's fun and easy to make a picture book. Magazines and catalogues are filled with pictures you can use.

A photo album
of your child's special days, family and friends.

Your child will enjoy his photo album forever.

A surprise book
with flaps to open and interesting things to feel and smell.

Your child will love making things happen.

... and I was SO happy to see you!

Your own stories
will be the ones she loves best of all – especially if they are about her or you!

It's a special story when it's a real story!

Books

Books of her very own

A favorite book is something to be looked at, read often and enjoyed always.

Your child will love having books of her very own.

Where to find books:

- public libraries
- garage sales
- used book stores
- friends

CHAPTER EIGHT

Create! Create! – Don't Hesitate

You can learn so much about your child and she can learn so much from you, when you:

- Allow your child to create in her own way
- Adapt the activity so that you can do it together
- Add information that will help your child learn

To succeed you will need to . . .

- Choose materials that are easy for your child to use

- Make sure you've got enough stuff for everyone

- Let your child help get things ready

- Limit the number of children to two or three

- Set up for clean-up

- Have your own spot and your own supplies

Creating together the 3**a** WAY

allow your child to create "art" in his own way

At first,

your child will be more interested in making a mess than making a picture.

Try to remember – the mess will wash off, but the experience will last!

Then,
your child will love
scribbling on paper
and playing with
playdough.

Funny bunny.

Later,

when your child has more muscle control, she'll draw simple "pictures" and may tell you about them.

Mommy, that's you and me at the party!

And still later,
she'll create her own
work of art and enjoy
sharing it with you.

Creating together the 3a WAY

adapting to share the creating means . . .

Create face to face

and make comments
that show you're interested

Oh, no! Your snake's going to get me!

Take turns

- have your own materials
- keep the conversation going

Mmmm! I like your drawing. Will you tell me about it?

add new ideas and words . . .

. . . while you're creating together

. . . when you share the clean-up

. . . and when the "art" is on show.

Create in Your Own Way

For example . . .

Playdough recipe

Here is an especially good recipe for homemade playdough:
- 3 cups white flour
- 3 cups water
- 2 tablespoons cream of tartar
- 2 cups salt
- 2 tablespoons oil

Mix all the dry ingredients in a large pot. Add water and oil. Mix well. Cook over medium-high heat, stirring constantly until very firm and hot. Roll out on a floured board or table; fold and knead (like bread dough) to the proper consistency.

Play Clay recipe

Ingredients for Play Clay:
- 1 cup corn starch
- 2 cups baking soda
- $1\frac{1}{2}$ cups cold water

Mix corn starch and baking soda together in a pot. Add the water; cook the mixture over medium heat. Stir until the mixture looks like moist mashed potatoes. Pour the clay onto a plate and cover with a damp cloth. When it has cooled, knead it like dough until it can stretch like plastic.

Speaking from experience . . .
- Use a small amount at a time and keep the rest in a plastic bag or container so it won't dry out.
- To prevent sticking, work on a piece of wax paper and dust your rolling pin, cutting knife and cookie cutters with flour or corn starch.
- When joining two pieces of clay, wet the spot where they meet and press firmly together. Use white glue to join dry pieces.
- For colored dough, add food coloring to the water before mixing.

At different times you can add

food coloring

sparkles

smelly things

rice

At different times you can bring out

rolling pin

potato masher

plastic knives/forks

toy animals
(some dressed up
in playdough)

boxes for houses

Creative Suggestions

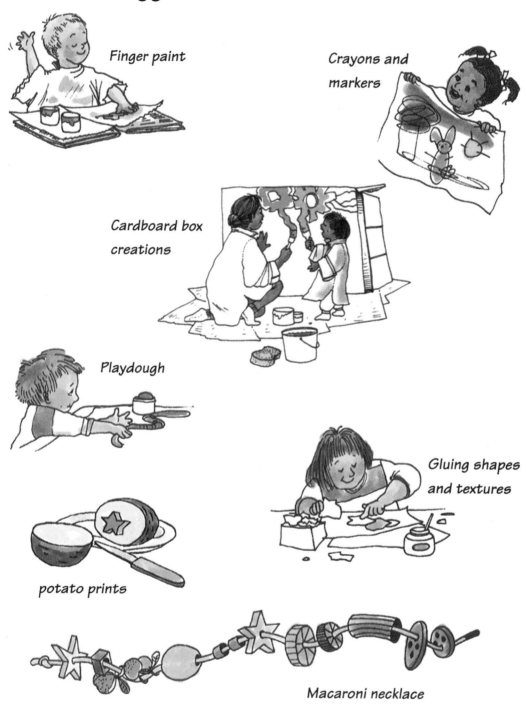

Finger paint

Crayons and markers

Cardboard box creations

Playdough

Gluing shapes and textures

potato prints

Macaroni necklace

CHAPTER NINE

Connecting Isn't Always Easy!

But It's Always Worth the Effort

Instead of going insane . . . 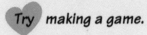 *making a game.*

**When you make the effort to connect the 3a WAY,
your child will:**

- listen to you because you listen to him
- feel like he belongs – rather than feel alone
- learn to trust – rather than mistrust
- learn to get along with others

All in a Day

When your child is whiny and demanding,
you can still connect . . .

Instead of tightening-up . . .   Try lightening-up!

Instead of saying "no" . . .   Try to go with the flow!

It's okay to say "no" when you have to, but . . .

Instead of just "no" . . .

Try to understand feelings . . .

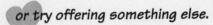*And then try wishful thinking . . .*

or try offering something else.

All in a Day

When your child is quiet and shy,
you can still connect . . .

Instead of being an entertainer . . .

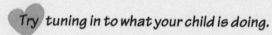 **Try** tuning in to what your child is doing.

Instead of giving up . . .

 Try being there to show you care.

Some children need more time to feel comfortable

Instead of despairing . . .

Try 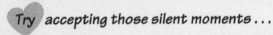 *accepting those silent moments . . .*

Try 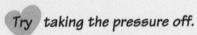 *sharing feelings . . .*

Try  *taking the pressure off.*

All in a Day

When your child only wants to do his own thing,
you can still connect . . .

Instead of going insane . . .    Try making a game.

Instead of feeling shut out . . .   Try joining in.

You can't always be close, but . . .

Instead of demanding more
and feeling sore . . .

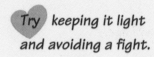 *keeping it light*
and avoiding a fight.

Instead of giving up . . .

 coming up with something new.

All in a Day

When your child is upset — you can't always make it better right away, but you can still connect . . .

Instead of ignoring feelings . . .   *Try* talking about them.

Instead of being disappointed . . .   Just know that some kids are more easily upset than others.

And generally in life . . .

Instead of insisting . . .   **Try** working things out.

Instead of dictating . . .   **Try** negotiating.

In Conclusion

YOU Really Do Make the Difference

Connecting with your child isn't always easy. But connecting the 3a WAY will always be worth the effort.

Be patient. Your child may not learn what you want him to learn right away. It may take a week, a month or maybe a year. In the meantime, because you are tuned-in to your child he will know that you love and care for him. And that's the most important thing for any child to know.